LEAD

PROVEN PRINCIPLES TO MULTIPLY
YOUR SUCCESS AT ANY LEVEL

SAM ADEYEMI

ACKNOWLEDGEMENTS

This book, which was first published under the title "Multiply Your Success: LEAD," has been revised to reach a global audience, and it has taken a team spread across continents to do the job. I am thankful to my dear protégé, Gregory Ijiwola, who had a ready answer for each request I made for contacts to handle different aspects of the publishing process. Rotimi Kehinde and the team at GodKulture Publishing did a great job with the editing and layout design especially with tight deadlines. And I appreciate the efforts of David Ayodele, our UK office manager, who worked with the graphic designers to come up with the cover, and Abel Bekele who manages our US office. Of course, this is building on the great work done on the first edition by the staff of Pneuma Publishing Limited.

I celebrate all the megastars in Daystar Christian Center who, by allowing me to experiment with all my lessons and ideas on leadership, have made it possible for me to multiply my potential for success. I am especially grateful to the pastors and leaders who have served with me selflessly on the faculty of the Daystar Leadership Academy whose names I am not listing only for the sake of space, and I am proud of the tens of thousands who have attended our programs and are making impact around the world.

I will always be grateful to God for my co-dreamer and charming wife, Nike, on whom I bounce almost all my ideas. She almost always has better ones though. The good thing is that I don't have to always explain where the ideas came from. And I appreciate our children, Sophie, David, and Adora, for their patience as I worked on another of my many projects.

CONTENTS

INTRODUCTION

*"No matter what your position or title is,
you have the ability to be a leader in your environment."*

When you hear the word "Leader" what comes to mind? For many, it is the picture of someone who occupies a position, especially in government. However, when we consider the world's population, or that of a country, it becomes obvious that only a few people will ever hold the title of president or prime minister in their lifetime. Does that mean that the rest of us do not have the ability to lead? How then can we describe the impact of parents, teachers, coaches and colleagues who help people to discover and to realize their potential everyday around the world?

The key concept in leadership is influence, which we all have in our daily environment. Leadership is the ability to influence people to achieve great goals. When you think about it, you have influenced other people either for good or for evil. You will find in this book, the ingredients that are needed to develop the ability to influence people positively. There are two dimensions to it: character and competence. As you develop them, your perspective to life will begin to change. You will begin to see opportunities where others see problems. As you acquire skills and solve problems, you will increase your influence on others.

Talking about solving problems, we all begin by dealing with our individual challenges. As we overcome them, we realize we do not have special problems. There are many in similar predicaments. As we deploy our skills and gifts to help them, greater opportunities for leadership come our way. It is not enough for you to succeed; you can multiply your success by guiding others to do what you do. That is another level of success altogether.

If you were raised in a culture similar to mine, leadership is perpetuated as being superior to one's followers so a change in the concept of achieving influence is necessary. The truth is you cannot fulfill your potential as a leader by dominating people. You can only rise to the highest level of success by committing yourself to serving people. It all begins with the ability to recognize people's needs. No matter what your title or position is, you can lead, right where you are. Welcome to a new level of success in leadership.

Chapter One

NEW VISIONS, NEW DREAMS

"One of the most critical factors in leadership is vision."

Without vision, we cannot inspire people to follow us. Whether you are leading a family, organization or nation, you must develop the ability to see people, places and things, not just as they are now but how they could be in the future.

Some of the world's notable visionaries have included Walt Disney, who imagined a theme park that families would come from all over the world to play and be inspired. He built the first one in California, and then had a bigger dream that resulted in Disneyland, Orlando, Florida. Although he was not present at the official opening of Disneyland Orlando having passed on, he had seen it in his imagination. His dream came to pass.

Another notable dreamer was Robert Woodruff who as President of the Coca-Cola Company led the company into global expansion at a time when people had doubts about the prospects of the company. We should add to the list Dr Martin Luther King Jr. who had a dream that there would be equal rights for people all colors in the United States of America. His dream is becoming a reality.

A young man at Harvard University had a dream at a time when computers were not used often. His dream was to make computers user friendly by installing programs that would make using the computer easier for everyone to use. Some people predicted that the concept of computers would soon fizzle out like other toys of that day. Bill Gates' dream has become a reality. In the process of fulfilling his dream, he became the richest man in the world.

Your only limitation is the limit of your ability to dream. Your vision is what you eventually become. Helen Keller lived a very wonderful life and became very successful. Though born blind, she was able to rise beyond her limitations to live a fruitful life. The foundation for improvement, change and progress is vision. Until our eyes see, our ears hear and our hearts grasp, things cannot move from the invisible world to the visible. There is a next level for you and this is a season of new visions and new dreams. You will receive yours. You will see something you have never seen before.

BUILDING CAPACITY FOR VISION

Prayer

One critical dimension to this unique ability of vision is prayer. We need to pray that God should remove limitations from our hearts and minds because there are certain things that make it difficult for us to have a vision. Either you have a vision or you don't. When God opens your eyes to see the future, you see possibilities. It is as real to you alone as the present day but it has not become reality. Once I see something clearly in my heart, I am bound to act on it because it is real.

If you are a leader and you cannot find time to pray and think, you may soon lose relevance.

Meditation

Meditation is the art of dreaming. Use your imagination to dream of possibilities. Travel into the future and make yours a world of possibilities. Dominate the unfavorable circumstances of your life through your imagination. Break free from your current limitations. In your imagination, you are not limited by time or space.

Your only limitation is the limit of your ability to dream.

If you are hungry and you have enough wisdom to begin to meditate on food, somewhere along the line, if you dream long enough, you will forget your hunger. What that means is you went into the future, borrowed satisfaction and brought it into the present temporarily. Of course, occasionally you will run into physical or natural challenges that will slap you in the face and attempt to distract you from your dream; but it is up to you to 'slap' that reality back and to protect your dream.

When you are not conscious of vision, which is what makes a person a leader, there will be no direction. The greatest threat to the survival of the average person is uncertainty of the future. It is the inability to know where to go and what to do today to make tomorrow better. That is why wherever you find a person who has developed the ability to capture a sense of vision for themselves and others, the person is like a magnet. Whether in a church, business, family, school, city or nation, he or she will attract people because people need vision to survive.

Exposure

Exposure to the right information also helps. Reading makes a whole world of difference. Just reading books on church growth by the pastor of the largest church in the world immediately after graduation helped me have a vision that I would pastor a large church. I was a jobless graduate, but I had a vision because I was reading something that sparked my imagination. God's Spirit took what I read and burned some pictures into my heart. My heart was hot as I was reading those books, listening to tapes and watching videos. Exposure matters. When a camera faces an object, as you press the shutter, the reflection of light on that object establishes an image on the film in the camera. Sometimes, during observation of someone's environment, your shutter opens and God uses natural phenomenon to burn pictures into your heart as He did for Abraham. He used the stars to burn the picture of children into Abraham's heart. Dream about your future. Get books, cut pictures from magazines, write checks in your name and stick them on the wall in your room. Advertise your future to yourself.

LIMITATIONS TO VISION

Past Failures and Painful Experiences

Our past failures and painful experiences have the tendency to erect barricades in our minds. For the average person who grows up in the developing part of the world, those past failures can include not getting an education because their family could not afford to pay for it. It can also include eviction from an apartment due to inability to pay rent, watching a loved one die because of lack of money or basic hospital equipment, going to bed hungry and so on. Beyond these, the loss of a job or jobs, breakdown in marriage, and business failure can create strongholds in our minds. However, your past does not have to dictate your future. Your tomorrow will be better than your yesterday.

Traditions

Sometimes, the methods used can cause a hindrance in our ability to innovate. Traditions have the power to inhibit your vision. I grew up hearing this saying: "Let us do it the way it has always been done so that we can get the results we have always been getting." I refuse to accept things the way they are. If you only maintain the status quo, you are not a leader. This statement, said to have been made originally by Albert Einsten, has encouraged me, "To do things the way they have always been done and to expect different results is one of the definitions of insanity.". It has given me a strong foundation for choosing to be radically different.

Being Self-Centered

Human nature is selfish. We want our problems solved first before others. That may make sense if you are in an aircraft that has lost cabin pressure. The safety instructions say that you should fix your own oxygen bag before you help somebody else. However, in leadership, it does not work that way. You succeed by solving problems for others. The kind of visions you get when you want to solve problems for an organization, city or nation are quite different from when your aspirations are to have food, clothes and a used car that you can call your own.

If you only maintain the status quo, you are not a leader.

I must point out that the more basic social services are absent in a country, the more its citizens are prone to strive to solve their own problems themselves. Their selfishness seems justified, and the quality of leadership drops. People then use positions of leadership as an opportunity to solve their own personal problems.

Inflexibility

Sometimes we are inflexible in our thinking. We are in love with our opinions. If you do not have a flexible mind, you cannot create the future. It is only in your imagination that God can give you a $5000 suit when you do not even have enough shirts yet.

Some people's thoughts are so opinionated, they cannot see the next level. Their thoughts are cast in concrete. However, some people have fluid thoughts and can imagine anything. Are you limitless in your capacity to dream? Can you see five loaves of bread and two fish feeding five thousand people with some leftovers? Can you see a lame person walk or blind eyes open? Can you see a desert becoming a city? Can you see a pauper becoming a CEO? How do you dream of owning a jet, when you have a small income? Your mind must be fluid not rigid.

Lack of Creativity

The ability to bring into existence what has never existed before is a nature we derived from God. In the biblical account of creation, God looked at the earth and it was without form and void, yet He saw the potential for light. He created you in His image so it is your destiny to have vision and to create things. Not only did He bring out land from the water, He brought plants and animals out of the soil. He did not bring any raw materials from heaven except vision[1]. Everything you need to fulfill your destiny is already around you, but you need vision to realize the potentials in your resources.

If you occupy any position right now, that is the best opportunity in the world. Use your imagination to create solutions to problems. Your creative ability is the secret to miracles. Jesus said that He saw miracles and healings in His imagination before He carried them out[2].

Inability to See Potentials

Still on the subject of vision, you can have vision concerning people. To succeed in leading people, you must have the capacity to see them not just the way they are but the way they could be. If you are a man or woman of vision, do not use people's pasts to judge them. Sometimes the worst drunk in town may become the greatest evangelist.

Everything you need to fulfill your destiny is already around you, but you need vision to realize the potentials in your resources.

People are naturally attracted to those who believe in them. Most people do not have faith in themselves. Moreover, many do not have someone who has faith in them. Can you see the good in people that they cannot see in themselves, or that others have not seen in them?

If I hold a mango seed in my hands, and I ask you 'what is this?' What would be your response? If you only see things the way they are, you will say it is a seed but if you also see things the way they could be, you will add that it is potentially an orchard of mangoes. Things will not always remain the way they are now. Change is coming to your family, organization and nation.

Small Dreams

Start from where you are presently, but do not stay there. It is not a crime to start small. If you can see the future, it is just a matter of time before you become that future. You must have a dream, because your dreams will become your reality. Everybody sees the same sky but not everyone sees the same horizon. Where people see scarcity, you can see abundance. Where people see pain, you can see healing.

Sometimes, our dreams are too small for God to use to do significant things in our lives. I remember several years ago, our church was negotiating to buy two or three plots of land to build a small facility. It did not work out and looking back, I am glad it did not. That was too small for our destiny. Some years later, I asked God, "How do we raise a hundred million Naira (about $800,000 at that time) for our building project?" He answered, "Don't build for yesterday; build for tomorrow, what you're asking for is too small." I increased the size of my dream. Eventually, when we got a facility, it was a very large one; five times that amount of money in value. Make it a habit to dream big.

Chapter Two

DEVELOPING LEADERSHIP QUALITIES

David, in the Bible, led ancient Israel by the integrity of his heart and by the skillfulness of his hands[1]. He had a combination of character and competence. When we talk of developing leadership ability, I think we need to focus on those two dimensions. Character is who you are, while competence is your ability to do what you do.

Competence

Based on the Parable of Talents, we learn that God gives each man responsibility according to his ability. If God gives you a particular project to manage, it is a reflection of your capacity at that time. This implies that when you pray for promotion, God expects you to develop the capacity to manage that promotion; else, you make it difficult for God to answer that prayer. No one puts new wine in old wineskins.

It will lead to a waste of resources. One of the most important skills we should develop in life is leadership ability.

John Maxwell, renowned motivational speaker and author, in his book, The 21 Irrefutable Laws of Leadership, says that the first law of leadership is "The law of the lid: you will never be more successful than your leadership ability will allow"[2].

Many believe that only a few are born to lead. When a leadership seminar is advertised, most people do not show up because they do not think they are leaders. Some people think that leadership is a complex topic. Simply stated, leadership is the ability to influence someone to say or do something. You have obviously influenced someone at one point or the other. Even children do it. You are a leader already! Everyone has the potential to lead. The big issue now is the extent to which you are developing that leadership ability.

You do not have to hold political office before you can influence a city or nation. Each of us can lead where we are until there is sufficient progress to change the entire system. I understand it takes only two percent of a community to change that community. Salt does not have to be the same quantity as food before it changes its taste. You do not have to wait until everybody in the organization or country commits to the new visions and values; you are sufficient enough to lead the process of change right where you are.

The development of leadership qualities is a priority in life. You must develop the ability to influence human beings. They are more difficult to deal with, but there are specific skills you can use. Anyone can learn to be a leader. Jesus trained ignorant and uneducated people for just three and a half years and the institution He started is still growing after two thousand years. The principles He taught are still the foundational principles used to run effective organizations, institutions and nations all over the world. It would help us to build on the same principles.

Most people like to believe that leaders are born. Though some people have natural traits that make leadership easy for them, the truth is 'leaders are made.'

Character

The force of character is evident in the life of David, the ancient king of Israel. His boss, Saul, became so jealous he decided to get rid of him. When he could not kill him in the palace, he took a battalion of elite soldiers and went after him. Somehow, things turned around and David was the one who had the opportunity to kill Saul; but he refused. David had a second opportunity. He walked into the middle of Saul's camp and came to the place where Saul lay sleeping. One of the young men with him said, "David, kill him." David said no. The young man said, "Let me strike him on your behalf, only once, not twice!" And again, David refused.

Each of us can lead where we are until there is sufficient progress to change the entire system.

David made a profound statement as it was a rare opportunity to train those young rebels who grew up fighting for survival. "Who will touch the Lord's anointed and be guiltless?" He said, "Leave him to God. If God wants him to die, he would either kill him at the battlefront or kill him in his sleep. Nobody will touch someone that God has anointed and remain guiltless." He took Saul's water bottle and his weapon and walked away. When he got to a far distance, he cried out and woke Saul and his assistants up. He did not hurt the man who was after his life[4]. Not seeking revenge is a function of character.

In considering the combination of character and skill, character comes first. Talent causes many to be swollen-headed, and the people who have the worst struggles with character development most times are gifted people. A gift or talent, being an act of God's benevolence, makes the achievement of success and fame to come easy. It is easy to take things for granted, or to think there is no point cultivating discipline or submitting to authority. I will rather consider faithfulness before ability. If someone is faithful, he can add ability with time. In fact, he will add ability to character because he will be able to stay long enough to learn how to do the job. If someone has the skill but no character, he will only be a sophisticated crook.

Integrity

Let me take a brief detour to explain what integrity is. I remember twelve years ago when I felt like my vision was so big but things were happening very slowly. I prayed to God to help me make an impact on a national level that year. Then I heard that small voice in my heart; "It will not take me five minutes to put the power on you and all those things will happen. However, your character is the foundation I am looking at before I bless you with success. I cannot give you success that you aren't ready for because you will crash. Build your character."

That was a very sobering experience for me. A couple of weeks later, God sent an elderly man to come talk to me. The message was I should hold on and keep the faith because my breakthrough was on the way. I should wait. The man stressed that it is hard to experience not being used by God when He has used you so greatly in the past. It is not good to retire before your season is over. Integrity is the foundation for enduring success.

Integrity is being perfectly honest with God, with others and yourself. I am choosing my words carefully. I did not say that having integrity is being a perfect human being, although we should strive towards perfection. Honesty is one of the qualities

Integrity is the foundation for enduring success.

that people value the most in a leader. You can have power to win a war or raise the dead; you may have a lot of charisma and oratory power, but without integrity, those things will not count. When it comes to getting respect and followers, honesty is the basic requirement. When our values change frequently with circumstances, it is a sign that we are not grounded in anything.

For a leader, there has to be a positive correlation between one's private life and one's public life. Do not teach what you are not doing. Do not lay heavy burdens on people that you are not willing to lift. Do not break the standards you enforce on others. Hypocrisy corrodes the credibility of a leader. It is important for leaders to be truthful. When leaders have integrity, what you see is what you get. They acknowledge their strengths and their weaknesses.

Usually, the first people to lose respect for a leader are those who are closest to him or her. It begins with the family, then neighbors, and then subordinates at work. Dishonest leaders breed dishonest followers. They breed "yes men" or "yes women" that tell the leader what they want to hear even if it is not the truth. When leaders have integrity, there is no need for pretense in public. All of us have the tendency to wear masks that we hide in our closets. We put different masks on depending on the side of us we want people to see at that time. Let us take those masks off.

Leaders that have integrity acknowledge their strengths as well as their weaknesses. Dr. David Cho pastors the largest single congregation in the world in Seoul, South Korea. Some aspects of his writings scared me when I began to read his books because there were parts of his books where he wrote about his mistakes. At that time, I thought, if you are a leader, especially in church, people expect you to be

Hypocrisy corrodes the credibility of a leader.

perfect so you have to do everything not to disappoint them. I felt like you had to cover up parts of your life that would have caused people to lose confidence in you. Then I read Dr. Cho's books and saw his openness. Now I could not fathom how the pastor of the largest church in the world could be so open about his mistakes in books knowing the books would be distributed all over the world.

There is a reason these stories had such impact on me. In the environment where I grew up, the leaders are never wrong. In fact, in the past, a king could not be wrong; he was not accountable to anyone. If he saw a very beautiful woman, he asked who she was and they said she was someone's wife, he would forcefully take her; and there was nothing her husband could do about it. Dictatorial or domineering leadership still permeates our political, social and spiritual institutions. Unfortunately, this kind of leadership does not depend on moral authority but on positional authority to exert influence. It depends on power or coercion to secure cooperation. In the long run, it is ineffective.

My experience with Dr. Cho's stories made me realize that admitting mistakes builds trust between the people and us. It also encourages them to deal with their own weaknesses. When leaders pretend to have no flaws, the followers think that when they get into leadership positions, they also have to pretend and become hypocrites. So the cycle of failure in leadership continues.

We can get professionals to brand and package us. We can be taught how to look, stand and conduct ourselves, which are important. However, we can focus so much on the outer man while our inner man is full of schemes, self-indulgence, lack of self-control and lust. There is a very powerful principle for leadership; "When you clean the inside, somehow the outside takes care of itself." In other words, when you take care of your character, your reputation will take care of itself. Ultimately, we never rise beyond the capacity or limit of our character.

Courage

Leadership requires bold decision-making and daring action. The one who wants to be a successful leader must develop courage. Courage is acting in the presence of fear. Once fear is completely absent, courage loses its definition. If you do not have fear then you do not need courage. The fear of failure is a natural phenomenon and a powerful emotion. It is an emotion that all of us have experienced at one time or another. However, what matters is what you do with fear. If you have had cause to be afraid about the turnout of a decision or an action, it is normal.

With courage, leaders take initiative; they do more of acting than reacting. They are proactive. Fear has the capacity to kill initiative. Once you get a group of people working together, there is a good synergy and they begin to produce results. Somewhere along the line, as you generate momentum, which is the power it takes to keep an object moving, things get easier. If fear shows up when you have already built momentum, you can crush it, but if you have not moved at all, fear paralyses initiative and kills creativity. I would suggest mastering the fear of failure instead of looking for a way of eliminating it completely from our lives. We should learn to master it. Fear keeps people from taking necessary steps to fulfill their destiny and no one is going to follow someone who is afraid to take the required steps.

Ultimately, we never rise beyond the capacity or limit of our character.

It takes courage to say what you need to say when you know some of the consequences may not be palatable. It takes courage to run against the crowd and to be the only one that is taking a stand on an issue. Our country is not changing fast enough because the average person has found it easier to follow the tide than to go against it.

Can you say 'no' when you know that the truth will hurt someone's feelings? How many of us have had to make difficult phone calls? With courage, we act in spite of our fears. As the saying goes, "Fortune favors the brave."

Developing Courage

You develop courage by taking action in the presence of fear. You will not know whether you will die or not until you jump. After seeing that bold action is not always fatal, you get used to acting in spite of your fears. Now, that will separate you from the pack by miles.

Can you stand alone on an issue? Sometimes, the people you lead may not understand the issues at stake. You do not have to listen to popular opinion all the time. I know there is the saying that, "The voice of the people is the voice of God." Sometimes, the voice of the people is the voice of the devil. You may have to make a choice between breaking principles and obeying the voice of the people. Which one will you choose: to stick by sound principles and suffer rejection or to get approval at all cost? Rejection can be very painful. However, successful leaders make unpopular decisions sometimes.

Have Divine Inspiration

To overcome fear and develop courage, you need to experience the inspiration of the Spirit of God. The Bible compares being full of God's Spirit with being intoxicated with wine. This is because when God's Spirit influences your thinking and your emotions, He raises you beyond fear. Why do people who commit crime take alcohol or drugs first? It is because when they are under such influences, they lose the emotion of fear

You may have to make a choice between breaking principles and obeying the voice of the people.

temporarily. However, while hard drugs may give a false sense of reality and solve emotional problems temporarily, they are destructive in the long run.

It is not every measure of the infilling of God's Spirit that can rid you of fear. Just like one little sip of alcohol is not likely to get you drunk. Sometimes, God's Spirit only has a minor influence in our lives, but when we are full of the Spirit, He can move as He did with David, a teenager who ran towards Goliath when trained solders were running away[5]. Courage brings unusual victories.

Focus On Your Destiny

When you define success by how much money and things you have, the loss of material things will threaten your sense of security. However, we may have to experience temporary loss to be able to make it to our destination. That is why Jesus told people who wanted to join His team; "Anyone who wants to come after me must deny himself and carry his cross"[6]. Some of the most successful leaders the world has seen had such great visions of the future they were willing to lay down their lives. When you are on that dimension, the obstacles that stop others cannot stop you from achieving your dreams.

You need to commit to do whatever it will take to achieve your dreams, whether it is easy or not. May I suggest here that there is the need for all of us to overcome the fear of failure? You must get rid of that fear. If you study success very well, you will know that you do not succeed without failing. By knowing that, you will welcome failure as a friend not as a threat. The fear of failure is one of the major reasons for failure because it will kill your initiatives and stop you dead in your tracks from attempting anything at all. I am not afraid to fail because every failure for me has become a learning experience. I have more respect for the person who tries and fails than for the person who has never failed because he did not attempt anything.

Dreams grow best in the fertilizer of failure. You can turn your failure into manure in which you plant the seed of a new dream. I have failed many times. I can write a good book on failure. In other words, I have tried many things that did not work, but I discovered that you could try ninety-nine ways that may not work for you, but one approach will eventually work out. The one that works will compensate for others that do not work.

Many do not take courageous action because they do not want to die, but as the saying goes, "Cowards die many times before their death." Those who act with courage and solve major problems for humanity do not die. Death for them is only a transition to a higher state. In any case, even when they are physically dead, we still 'hear their voices' on earth. Their ideas never die.

I have a challenge for the man of the house who is not taking bold steps for the family; you need to understand you did not marry just for the sake of marrying and giving birth to children. God has a stake in that family and there is a destiny to fulfill. If you need to start a business, start it. If you need to take a job, take it. Act in spite of your fear; whatever it requires, make sure you overcome fear.

We must lead our families, organizations and nations with courage. We must dream big and commit to the fulfillment of our dreams. We must stand with conviction for principles and the highest values at whatever cost. Generations after us will be grateful for our investment.

Chapter Three

THE PRICE OF LEADERSHIP

Commitment

Success comes only to people who are committed to their dreams, objectives and assignments. Leaders who succeed in their callings in politics, business or church ministry are always people who have staying power. They are willing to do whatever it takes to see their objectives achieved. There is no point following someone who is not willing to stay with an assignment to the end.

Jesus said, "No one, having put his hand to the plough, and looking back, is fit for the kingdom..."[1]. God does not use people who are not dependable. I encourage you as a budding leader, if you want to accomplish great goals, you must commit to finish whatever you start.

You have to be very persistent. You must develop the ability to stick with one thing until the assignment is finished. Perseverance is not an inherited trait; it is cultivated and developed over time. You will always confront discouraging situations as a leader but you have to learn to be like a postage stamp. When you put it on an envelope, it stays with the envelope until it gets to its destination.

How to Develop the Quality of Commitment

Some people only get involved in very important assignments while some others are committed. They are two different things. There is a famous saying; "In the business of making bacon and eggs, the chicken is involved but the pig is committed." Their involvement in this statement are on two different levels; if you eat the egg, it does not cost the chicken its life. The chicken lays the egg but continues to live; but for you to eat the bacon, the pig dies. In the pursuit of a vision, some people are only involved while others are committed. Those who are committed will achieve the highest level of success. This commitment is critical to our ability to influence the entertainment industry, the educational system, science and technology, and the political and economic spheres in our nation. Each of us must pursue our goals with strict conviction until we achieve our dreams.

Always count the cost

"For which of you, intending to build a tower does not sit down first and count the cost..."[2]. Counting the cost today is a profession known as Quantity Surveying. People go to the university to learn how to value and assign a price to every item in a project when the design is complete. You can decide to adjust the building design if you do not have enough resources to pursue the project. Always do an assessment of what it will take to achieve your objective, and do not start what you cannot finish.

When I decline an invitation to speak, sometimes people say to me, "Please come, even if it is just for twenty minutes." I used to think that was not a lot of time anyway, so I would agree, but I eventually realized that it took more than just twenty minutes. It also cost me study time and travel time, or precious moments I should have spent at an event at my children's school. Now I take my time to factor in everything it will cost. Once I make up my mind to do it, it will be difficult for any excuse to stop me.

For you to be CEO of an organization, or Governor, or President, you must look beyond the title and prestige. Calculate what it will cost you to get there and what it will cost you to lead. Then be willing to pay the price for your prize.

Sacrifice

You can live your life on two levels. At the first level, you focus on what you can get out of life. On the other level, you focus on what you can give. Being a giver puts you on a higher pedestal than being a receiver. It is more blessed to give than to receive[3]. This is why many people do not succeed in leadership. They are self-centered. Leadership costs. It requires sacrifice. Do not be deceived; you do not get something for nothing. Success requires hard work, and investment is the key to achievement.

...Be willing to pay the price for your prize.

Is it not interesting how sometimes it looks like things are actually working much more easily for some other people? We wish we were living their lives. The grass may seem to be greener at the other side, but has it ever occurred to you that it is so because someone is weeding it? No one succeeds without paying a price. Anything that is of value in this world has a price tag on it. Success in life is a prize that has a price.

I mentioned while speaking somewhere recently that I came to Lagos, Nigeria, some years ago with nothing. My salary was 600 Naira (about $90 then) a month.

Some people's eyes popped open and were amazed at what they just heard; I could see that I had gotten their attention. They could not have imagined what I said to be true. People see where I am now in life, but they cannot contemplate how I got here.

Before you quit your present job, please ask yourself a few questions. Why do you want to move? Why do you want to abandon your project? Why are you going to abandon that relationship? Hold on! Are you assuming that there is a perfect relationship, husband, wife, friend or church somewhere? You may be accepting a false reality. Is it simply because you want to escape some hardship? Some hardship and suffering may be part of your training. You need to have a positive attitude. If you move, will you compromise some principles and your core values? It is important for you to seek wise counsel from people who have navigated their own paths and paid the price to become leaders.

As a leader, you need to give up for you to go up. Some of the people who have built successful businesses sometimes could not even take a dime while paying salaries of employees. This is a cost to move to a higher level. Do not think that it is having the biggest car or house, or having the largest amount of money that makes you a leader. It is paying the greatest price. If you are not willing to die for your cause, you will not really live it either.

Criticism

Being a leader will attract critics. Leadership usually positions you where every other person can see your weaknesses. Every aspect of your life will be of interest to people. They will make many assumptions about your decisions. You must have a healthy self-esteem to manage criticism. You must be able to bear the hurt while looking for the wisdom in what was said, or else you will be distracted. It is just a part of the game.

Loneliness

Sometimes leadership causes loneliness. The life of a leader is a whole new ball game. Once you become a leader, you find it difficult to share your most intimate issues with everyone. Many around you will not be able to see from your perspective. This is because all they can see are the privileges that you enjoy. They cannot put themselves in your shoes. They do not understand your fears and hurts. It is better for you to keep quiet sometimes than to talk. It is part of the price for leadership.

Opposition

Leadership also attracts opposition. When you are unknown, nobody cares about the kind of clothes you put on or the type of car you drive. When you occupy a leadership position, everybody wants to use you as toothpick. You have to count the cost before you commit to the awesome assignment of leading your city or country out of poverty and backwardness. Leadership initiates change, which threatens the survival of those who have thrived on existing economic or political structures. Expect some resistance, and plan to overcome it with persuasion and the right attitude.

Obedience

I learned a big lesson in obedience a few years ago when my church was trying to move out of our former location. We were there for years, running five services on Sunday mornings, and we could not find a new location. One day I was praying and said, "Lord, do something; open up a way for us. We are not making progress." God responded, "Your definition of progress is different from mine. Progress for you is always forward motion, but progress to Me is for you to do whatever I want you to do in my time, including standing on the same spot." I said, "Lord I am sorry, we are making progress."

Whenever people travel within the United States on vacation, they always rent a car with a GPS navigation system. When programmed, it tells you where you are, where you are going, how long it will take you to get there and the distance. It will also tell you to proceed to the nearest road. It sounds like divine guidance because God said you would hear a voice behind you telling you where you should go, whether you should turn to the left or to the right.[4]

Expect some resistance, and plan to overcome it with persuasion and the right attitude.

Sometimes, if I do not hear anything after driving for some distance, it would seem something has gone wrong with the box. That is how we are sometimes. Just because you have gone three months without receiving a new idea does not mean that God is far away. It does not mean that you are not making progress; it does not mean that you are off-course. Stay with the last instruction. We all have that compass in our conscience to guide our steps.

How can I decide to turn right when the navigational system has not given such a directive when I am driving in a city I have never been before? All of us are on a journey; we are on a path that we have never walked before. We have never lived this life before; it is our first time here. We do not know the route. One person does and the only thing that counts in terms of direction is His voice. I earnestly encourage you to commit to obeying that inner voice.

There is no future in any position or in any location. Not all that glitters is gold. Your future is rooted in revelation. When the Lord is your shepherd, you will not fail.

Chapter Four
PRINCIPLES
OF VISION

Vision is the essence of leadership. It is the capacity to perceive or see. It is vision that makes a leader. As Bill Hybels said, "Take vision away from a leader, and you cut out his or her heart"[1]. Leadership is the ability to secure cooperation from people to achieve a powerful goal. It is the capacity to see what others cannot see, to recognize potentials in people, circumstances, and places. It is seeing people and things not just the way they are but the way they could be, and championing improvement.

Vision practically alters your life; it restructures you from the inside and turns you into a magnet. When people come around you, they begin to get a sense of direction for their lives and a sense of assurance about the future. You cannot get that assurance everywhere; you can only get it from someone who has the capacity to perceive the future. That is how it works. People need direction and leadership.

Anyone who can make it happen in his imagination has done it. This is because what he sees inside today, he will see on the outside tomorrow. It is a principle. The man who achieves great goals in his imagination will carry himself differently from the one who only lives in the present. In essence, he has tasted food that his contemporaries have not smelled. He is dancing to music others cannot hear. He is living in another world. His speech, attitude, and carriage cannot be the same as the person who has not been there.

In life, what you see is what you get. Do not ever lose grip of that basic truth about vision. You must have access to vision and turn that vision to reality. A leader must be a winner to attract followership. It is not enough to tell us that this is where we are going or this is what the future is going to be like. You need to tell us how to get there and we need to know that you know how to get there.

How to Fulfill Your Vision

Become the Person in the Vision

When you look at that great dream of your future, you will realize that the most important factor in it is you. You are the magnet that will attract everything else in the picture. To make the vision happen, we must put enough power in the magnet. To put it more clearly, you must grow to the size of your vision. You must become the person in the vision. To grow physically, you have to eat. Likewise, it is information that grows your heart. Learn the things that will give you capacity to function as the person in the vision. Read books, take classes and get mentoring.

Develop a Plan

A vision is essentially a picture of the destination. However, you need to figure out how to make the journey from where you are to where you want to be. That begins with you setting specific targets or goals. Usually, your vision describes a future state that is very different from your current realities. It can be so overwhelming that you may not be able to design the grand plan for accomplishing it. But, you still need to develop a systematic plan for it to be accomplished. Begin where you are. You may only be able to plan for one year. Go ahead. Before that year is over, you will be able to see further into your vision.

Grow People to the Size of the Vision

If your vision is big enough, you will not be able to achieve it alone. That is why you need to be a leader. Since you will have to secure the cooperation of others to fulfill your vision, the people on your team will influence the success of your venture. Give them self-esteem, train them and delegate to them.

Use Principles as Leverage

If your vision is big enough, you will not be able to achieve it alone.

Principles are unchanging truths or universal facts. Our world is under the control of principles. The more you understand those principles and satisfy their conditions, the more control you have in our world and getting your dreams and aspirations fulfilled. Principles are external road maps. If you are travelling, you do not need to invent your own map, especially if you do not know where you are going. The best thing to do is get an authentic road map and follow the directions. That is what principles are, they give us directions, and they make decisions easy for us.

When a leader sees a powerful vision, he soon realizes he does not have the power to make the vision happen. The leader then turns to principles, because we can leverage on principles to achieve amazing results. What do I mean? Let's assume I have a small quantity of corn seeds; my vision helps me to see the potential harvest in my few corn seeds. How do I translate my sight from seed to harvest? I use the principle of sowing and reaping. I did not create the principle; I met it here. Yet I cannot deny its existence. I cannot make a seed grow, but God has invested the power to make a seed grow in nature. I choose to align with principles and use them to multiply the little resources that I have.

The person who trivializes the importance of principles is in for many struggles in the bid to achieve success. Refusal to use principles to achieve results breeds desperation, manipulation, intimidation and ultimately frustration.

Use Your Mind as Leverage

Your mind is your number one asset and you can leverage on it to achieve outstanding success. "As he thinks in his heart so is he,"[2]. With some small changes, you can create massive changes in the circumstances of your life. I have stopped running after circumstances, trying to make them change; I have seen too much frustration that way. I have discovered that the race is not to the swift, and the battle is not to the strong[3]. Renewing the mind is the key to transformation. Leverage is the big word.

Adopt Principles as Personal Values

Now, there are many principles. When you get to study them, you will realize that there are specific principles that will aid the fulfillment of your vision. When you adopt those principles and you internalize them, they become your own personal principles; what we call your core values. Values are different from principles. Values are subjective while principles are objective. Values are personal opinions rather than facts or evidence. When you adopt a principle and make it a personal value, it means that principle now governs your emotions and feelings. It means you have so internalized the principle that it has become part of your life. The principles you adopt become your personal standards. Principles have no respect for how you feel. They never change; they remain the way they are.

Loving people, being honest and being financially prudent are things you should do, not because the law requires you to do them but because they are part of your personal standards.

Use Principles to Solve Problems

In the course of being a leader, you will come across diverse situations and circumstances. As a pastor, I have had the opportunity to deal with all sorts of situations and circumstances. When I was younger, I would hear someone's challenge and say to myself; "it cannot get worse than this." In time, I learned to accept that whenever I thought a situation was bad, it was only a matter of time before I heard of something worse. As a leader, when you come across these issues, you are able to use principles to deal with them with consistency. The principles you adopt decide your responses before the circumstances happen. Decision-making is easier and faster.

When you do not base your decisions on principles to achieve your vision, you will rely on shortcuts, quick fixes and get-rich-quick schemes.

When you do not have principles that guide your decisions as a leader, you cannot be objective. Your decisions will be subjective, largely determined by feelings or sentiments.

Some societies and cultures place very little value on principles. When you do not base your decisions on principles to achieve your vision, you will rely on shortcuts, quick fixes and get-rich-quick schemes. This lack of alignment with principles makes us subject to creating short-term solutions for long-term problems.

We place too much value on money and material things; in fact, that is society's definition of success. We do not care how people get money, as long as they can get it. Our definition of breakthrough is for someone to become wealthy quickly. It is a mindset that is sweeping our culture. So today, we have a society where people make money without working or applying the principles of wealth creation.

Some seem not to know the essence of a constitution. A constitution is a document that contains the vision and the principles that will guide the fulfillment of the vision of a nation. When this is not understood in a nation, the first set of people to break principles will be leaders and law enforcement officers. It should be the number one assignment of leadership to enforce principles; there is no other way to fulfill your vision legitimately.

Infallibility of Principles

To be realistic, we do not break principles. It is principles that have the power to break us. This is why I read a lot. Through reading, I discover the principles and practices that have made success possible for others. By the discovery and application of certain principles, the dreams I tried to accomplish unsuccessfully some few years back have become possible.

I remember the day I approached Dr. David Oyedepo and said, "Sir, what do you do if the church refuses to grow?" I had tried everything I knew. When you try everything and nothing is working, it means you need to know a little bit more. I will never forget his response. He said, "Whatever it is you are doing, continue to do it. Growth is seasonal. As long as the farmer continues to sow his seed, he does not actually have a problem, because some day the power of God will kick in and turn his seed into a harvest. The real problem happens when the farmer becomes frustrated because he is not seeing immediate results and he stops sowing seeds. When the farmer stops sowing seeds, there is nothing for God to grow into a harvest." My mentor knew that my frustration came because I was not aligned with the principle, so he taught me to align with the principle that controls growth and development.

Application of Principles

Until we align with principles, we cannot tap into the power that God has reserved for us for the achievement of great visions. Do you see how it works? You begin with the application of principles in your life. That is what I did. When things became difficult and I became desperate, I sensed that I had a great destiny but was not getting anywhere near fulfilling it. Then I began to research. I started reading books on how to succeed. I made exciting discoveries. As I applied them to my life, things changed for me. Then I realized that most people in our country were also struggling to succeed. That gave me the opportunity to influence many lives.

The starting point therefore is for you to apply the principles to your life, and secondly, to apply the principles to your relationships. It begins with your family. I never knew how to socialize; I was a chronic introvert. I did not even know how to start a conversation; and even if you started it, I did not know how to keep the conversation going. How can you be a leader and influence people if you cannot communicate your thoughts? I began to read books where I learnt relationship principles. Testing them on people was an exciting experience.

My brother, who is also a minister, has a different temperament from mine. He is very friendly and sociable. When we were growing up, I cautioned my brother several times to be more focused and serious minded. Yet, when I began to read books on leadership, I saw that his personality traits fit the characteristics of a leader better. I was the one who needed to learn to be nice and friendly. Now some people who do not relate to me personally see me on stage and think I am an extrovert. When I tell people that I do not like to talk, they do not believe it. I am applying the principles I have learnt.

Apply Principles to Organizations

When I speak to business owners in Nigeria, I ask how many businesses founded by Nigerians are a hundred years old? I have been asking this question for several years and I am still searching. I use that question to draw their attention to a cultural problem. The life view in most parts of Africa does not align with principles that make life predictable. There is greater belief in unverifiable myths. The world, in that view, is under the control of some overwhelming and invisible forces, and is therefore unpredictable. This is why most people do not build their lives and organizations on principles.

They value friendship over business. When they want to recruit staff, they hire someone because he is a nephew or cousin, not because he or she qualified for the job. Such people are sometimes the most difficult to fire because relatives will come and plead with the business owner to change his mind. Then the person becomes a liability to the company. Until you manage your business in such a way that family members are employed based on competence, and can be fired when they break rules, you cannot succeed in business.

Effects of Principles

Paradigm Shifts

The discovery of principles results in a paradigm shift for a leader. Many things in life are unpredictable. On the other hand, principles make life predictable. They are fixed. They do not move for circumstances and people, people and circumstances move for them.

There is an old urban legend of a captain who was piloting a ship at night which I will paraphrase. The captain saw another ship far-off, or at least he saw a light. He went on the radio, got the frequency of the other ship, and said, "I am coming in that direction, move." The person speaking from the other end replied, "You are the one that has to move." This man said again, "I am captain. This is the name of this vessel, I am set on this course and I'm not going to change course, you are the one that must change course." The voice on the radio insisted, "You are the one that must change course; I am not going to move." With anger, the captain said, "I am giving you the last warning now. I am the captain of this ship and this is the name of this vessel, move now." Then the man at the other end said, "Well, I am the man in charge of the light house." A lighthouse is a tall round tower with a powerful light that stands in the middle of a river or sea to guide sailors. The man thought it was a ship, but the moment he heard that it was a lighthouse he quickly changed course.

When you shift your paradigm in alignment with principles, you experience transformation and you get better results.

I am trying to make a point. Your personal beliefs are formed largely by the experiences you have had over time. Some women, for example, believe that all men are the same; while some men hold the view all women are the same. Some hold certain beliefs about specific nationalities. They believe some are not to be trusted, some are not tidy, some love money and so on. Now those are not principles, they are just opinions and prejudices. However, when you come across a principle like love, you realize it is not going to change; you are the one that has to change.

If you decide to plant your seed in the wrong season, it will not grow. If you choose to align with the principle and plant at the right season, you get a harvest. When you shift your paradigm in alignment with principles, you experience transformation and you get better results. Those results inspire people to follow you.

Unusual Results

Leaders are winners. When people want to know how you are succeeding, that is your opportunity to influence them. You can give them a new vision of themselves and their circumstances.

When you teach principles with proof, people will listen. I have proof for the principles I teach. When I have to speak to an unfamiliar audience, I have learnt to start with my story. When people see the gap between where I was and where I am now, they listen with intense attention to hear how I crossed my bridges. A leader attracts followership through inspiration. When you apply principles with results, you inspire others to release their potentials.

If you have experienced changes in your life through the application of principles, especially in the developing part of the world, people need to hear your voice now. Many around us do not know how to change their lives and to live their dreams. Young people need to know that there is a better way to pass examinations rather than cheating. They can rise above the pressures of their harsh environment and not give in to desperation. Problems are actually opportunities depending on our perspective. People often do not know how to succeed on their jobs, manage their businesses or how to treat employees. You need to help people discover what works, and to inspire them to act with courage.

Chapter Five
LEADERS
AND PRINCIPLES

Some people believe in luck. They believe that this world is under the control of some extraneous and overwhelming forces that man should not bother to control. That tends to kill the rational part of their brains. They are unable to do things they should do to exercise control over their environment and circumstances. This irrational thinking has laid the foundation for our belief in luck or fate. Because success by these means is so rare, there is a tendency to think that the few people who achieve success only make it by a stroke of luck. That mindset must be abandoned.

When success does not rest on principles, it is temporary. It is like building a house on sand. The house stands when the weather is favorable. However, when bad weather comes, the house will collapse. The person who builds on principles has no fear when the wind is blowing. It does not matter whether the weather is favorable or not.

All those building their lives and pursuits on unstable ground will have to look for you when instability comes into their lives. So when your life is built on principles, your sense of security, success and worth comes from inside.

There are different kinds of leadership.

Leadership by Coercion

This kind of leadership uses intimidation and domination; it uses fear to get people to comply. It depends practically on the authority provided by a position. Outside a specific position with the title and power attached, this kind of leadership is useless.

When success does not rest on principles, it is temporary.

There is a classic story of how not to lead in the Bible. Solomon, the wise and wealthy king died, and Rehoboam, his son, became king. As soon as Rehoboam was made king, he had a discussion with the people; and the leaders of the people raised some issues. "Your father started well but somewhere along the line, he began to impose heavy taxes on us. These duties are too heavy a burden. Reduce these taxes and we will serve you. We will work with you and make your reign a peaceful and prosperous one" (author's paraphrase). Rehoboam replied, "Give me three days and I'll give you a response."

Rehoboam went to the people who had counseled his father, and asked, "How do I respond to these people?" The mature people said, "Sir, speak kindly and gently to them. Promise them you will serve them; lighten their burden and win their cooperation. If you do, these people will serve you forever." Then he approached his friends; people who had never held leadership positions and asked them, "How do I respond to these people?" They said, "Do you know who you are and what it means to be king?" Their focus was neither on the people nor service. Their emphasis was on his position, the power derived from that position and the fact that the essence of power was to dominate people. They said, "Don't spare them. If you speak softly, they will think you are a weak leader. Speak harshly to them; exercise that power."

Rehoboam stood before the people and said, "You said that my father was harsh, you haven't seen anything yet. My little finger will be thicker than my father's waist. He scourged you with whips. I will scourge you with scorpions." He got the surprise of his life that his foolish friends had not told him could be the result of leadership by coercion.

As soon as he had given his response, some of the leaders of the people told him; "King Rehoboam, you don't realize that you are the leader because we decided to follow you." Then they shouted to everyone to go home. He thought it was a joke. When he sent the head of treasury to collect taxes, they beat the man and killed him. They seceded. Ten out of twelve tribes in Israel cut off and formed a new country[1]. This was the result of leadership by coercion.

If you grew up in an environment where this type of leadership was all you experienced, the tendency is that by default, wherever you find yourself in a position of leadership that is what you will be prone to do. You must consciously work against this approach.

Leadership by Negotiation

This approach uses the resources of the position to win favor from followers. This is the style of an insecure leader with ulterior motive, who wants to use his or her position to acquire wealth or power. This person negotiates with the people he or she is leading. It is a marketplace principle: give the people what they want; you do not have to give them what they really need. However, people's expectations are sometimes too low, especially where they have been raised in deprivation.

The unfortunate thing about this kind of leadership is that it can mortgage the future of a family, an organization or a nation just for someone to occupy a leadership position. When you have a leader who is insecure and does not want to lose approval, then you have a big problem. Such a person craves for the acceptance of people at the expense of the future.

I have observed that in most developed economies, individuals are empowered to prosper. They give their governments a fraction of their wealth in the form of taxes, for the common good. Whereas, in most of the world, it is very difficult for the average citizen to live the kind of life their leaders live. Government becomes the biggest business. Citizens are impoverished and their basic needs are used to manipulate them. It is leadership by negotiation.

Leadership by Principles

Each time you do the right thing, your moral authority increases.

Our world is under the control of principles. The first quest of a leader is to find out basic principles that control our world, and then to leverage them to achieve results. Aligning with those principles may be tough, but it pays at the end.

The highest principle in relationships is love. It may be hard to love if you have experienced rejection and bitterness, and have had to fight for any little progress you made in life. One of God's commandments is, "Love your neighbor as yourself"[2]. You may not have been used to forgiving others all your life but you need to break those old negative habits. Rely on God to give you the power to forgive. Even if you feel like you are going to die, forgive anyway. That is the starting point. Each time you do the right thing, your moral authority increases.

Benefits of Leadership by Principles

Predictability

Principles produce predictability, which earns trust, honor and respect. When you have adopted powerful principles as your life values, your response in specific situations and circumstances will be predictable. When you have not adopted specific values, your responses to different circumstances will be unpredictable, and it is difficult to trust a person that is not predictable.

The person who leads with principles earns moral authority and does not need to force, intimidate, or create fear in people and remind them of his or her title.

Ethical Conducts

When you have built your life on principles, one thing is evident; you live by ethical standards. You may have told a lie before to avoid shame, but you now choose to speak the truth always knowing that lying will eventually make you lose credibility. It is not always easy to do the right thing but you choose to do it anyway.

Paul the Apostle, gave an encouragement to men; "Husbands, love your wives"[3]. Now, that is profound. It rests on the highest principle that guarantees success in relationships, which is love. Someone asks; "What if she is nagging me to death?" Love her all the same. Paul also encouraged women; "Wives, submit yourselves to your own husbands"[4]. Will a woman feel like yielding to her husband's leadership all the time? I bet not! At times, some husbands act like they are ignorant. Even then, we do not act crazy because someone else is acting crazy. Love solves all problems.

We all have crucial financial needs sometimes and we have different ways we could make money. However, there are ethical ways to make money. Begging, borrowing without the capacity to pay, or misappropriating funds will cause a leader to lose credibility. In the Bible, Prophet Elisha declined the offer of a financial gift from Naaman, the Syrian Army General, after healing him of leprosy. He was not desperate or greedy for money. Gehazi, his assistant, was not principled enough; he thought that Elisha was foolish by not taking the money. He ran after Naaman and collected the gift. When he came back, Elisha said something to this effect, "As you collected the gift, you also collected the leprosy the man left behind"[5].

In order to exercise maximum influence as leaders, we must apply the principles of wealth creation and get our financial needs met through legitimate means. This must apply to all our endeavors also. Samuel, one of the prominent prophets in

When people see that you have needs, and you refuse to beg, it earns you honor.

the Bible stood before the whole of Israel and said, "If there is someone here whose property I took illegitimately, let the person speak up."[6] No one did. I find that action so inspiring. It is the height of integrity.

When people see that you have needs, and you refuse to beg, it earns you honor. When you speak, your words carry authority. It causes you to have influence with people. In fact, people love you. To some extent, people become passionate about helping you and following you to achieve goals. You do not need to intimidate or dominate anybody. This is principle-centered leadership.

Basic Principles for Success in Leadership

Love

Love helps you to appreciate the worth of others. It helps you to recognize their potential and to want to add value to them. Whatever work you do, you do it as if you are doing it for God. Whatever you do for man, you are actually doing for God because every human being is an extension of God. This attitude changes everything. When love is absent, greed, envy, selfishness, malice, rejection, hatred and such vices manifest in abundance. People succeed at the expense of others.

When leaders do not love the people they lead, it causes the spread of the cancer of self-centeredness in the system. People do not believe that their leaders are genuinely interested in their welfare. The way leaders treat people is the way people also treat one another.

Love empowers a leader and increases his or her influence. Love opens you up to creativity. When you feel that someone deserves the highest quality of life, you would begin to get ideas on how to make it happen.

I pray that God will open your eyes to recognize the unique opportunities you have to make impact on people's lives. There are some heavy-duty visions that God wants to drop into people's hearts that will transform communities and whole nations; visions that will turn people into multi-billionaires in the next few years, but the key to conceiving such dreams is compassion. Loving people has changed everything for me. If I find anything that is useful to the people I lead, I share them willingly. I do that because I have applied these truths and gotten results. If I do not share them with all the deprivation that I see around me, I would be a hypocrite. You must have love.

Love will empower you to prefer others and focus on giving, not getting. Love lets you stay on a queue respecting the time of the person who arrived earlier. You yield the right of way to someone who wants to merge into your lane. It makes you wait patiently for people to walk across the road at a pedestrian crossing. Ultimately, love motivates a genuine sacrifice for the good of others. On the other hand, the lack of love creates a "poverty mentality," making you so defensive in case somebody attempts to cheat you.

One word that describes the act of love is the word 'Respect.' Everyone deserves a measure of respect. We should use the words 'Sir' and 'Madam' generously not minding the status of the person being addressed. Sometimes we despise people who offer basic services. Therefore we have unemployed college graduates who are unwilling to offer basic services; but there is dignity in labor. It is better for someone to work and earn a living legitimately than to steal. We should respect anyone who has chosen that higher moral ground even if he is on a low-paying job.

Using courtesies like 'please', 'excuse me' and 'thank you' are further manifestations of love for fellow human beings. Showing love builds esteem, and that is one of the best gifts a leader can offer.

Vision

There is a connection between vision and love. Love is the basic principle for success in whatever you do. You cannot have the capacity for vision as a leader if you do not love people. Feeling strongly that people deserve to live a better life releases your creative juices. If you do not have love in your heart, hatred will blind your eyes. If you have any dream of the future at all, they will only create nightmares for those you lead.

Henry Ford, a mechanic, after he had developed the engine that runs on gas, began to manufacture and sell cars, but only rich people could buy his cars. Then he suggested to his directors that they make cheaper cars. His directors did not buy into his idea. They were making a good profit and there was no need to change something that was "working." Ford resigned from the first company he founded and started another

You cannot have the capacity for vision as a leader if you do not love people.

one. They began to produce the Ford model T, a cheaper version. As the legend goes, one day, he announced that they were increasing production to one thousand cars per day. His directors were concerned, wondering who would buy the cars. But his desire was for every family in America to be able to afford a car. That was love. Money was not his motivation. He wanted to make life more convenient for people. The more compassion he had, the bigger this vision grew.

Being Teachable

A leader can only go so far without being humble. No one knows everything. Being open to new information and wisdom, sometimes from one's subordinates will prevent us from being blind-sided. It is amazing that Naaman, the Army General we mentioned earlier, got the idea of healing from his leprosy from a maid. Successful leaders listen. They ask and receive advice. They are lifetime learners.

Self-control

We cannot control our external world until we can control our internal world. The most powerful form of government is self-government. The wise king, Solomon, once said; "He who is slow to anger is better than the mighty; and he who rules his spirit than he who takes a city"[7]. Self-discipline is one of the major characteristics of a leader. Lack of discipline causes a leader to lose his or her influence.

The appetites for food, drink, sleep and sex are legitimate; but when we violate God's laws to satisfy ourselves, or we become addicted to these appetites, we lose our moral authority. We must learn to ask God to help us to overcome habits and weaknesses that have the ability to frustrate our potential for success as leaders.

Chapter Six
CHARACTERISTICS OF PRINCIPLE-CENTERED LEADERSHIP

Ⓛ

Principle-centered leaders succeed

When you align with principles, you will succeed. A house built on sand may look exactly like the one built on rock. There are people who look like they are successful but they are not. It's only a matter of time. I want to scream into the ears of any young person who wants to make something of his or her life, "Don't cheat on exams, it will catch up with you someday." If those two people building houses started at the same time, who do you think will finish first? The man who built his house on the sand would finish first. The one building on the rock would have to dig deep. While he is still digging the foundation, his friend would be laying down his roofing. I encourage you, dear reader, not to let people around you who are cheating and flaunting their wealth confuse you and put you under pressure. You cannot win against principles in the long run.

Principle-centered leaders have unseen forces working to their advantage. When you sow a seed in the soil, invisible forces engage the seed and turn it into a tree. Every time you satisfy the conditions of a principle, nature releases power to aid you. Moreover, just as it is certain the season of harvest will follow after you sow; it becomes certain that you will succeed. It is no longer a matter of chance.

As a leader, I have discovered the power in planning. I have learnt to set goals; short-term, medium-term and long-term. I learnt that planning is winning. I have experienced it. I have also discovered the power in synergy. Two people will achieve together much more than the sum of what they will achieve separately. I have tasted the power in service. The more I have sought to serve people, to meet their needs with my gifts and skills, the more blessed I have become. Principles work.

Every time you satisfy the conditions of a principle, nature releases power to aid you.

Principle-centered leaders have success that lasts

When you lean on principles to achieve success, your success is not a matter of chances. You know exactly how you got to where you are and all you have to do is to continue to do whatever you did. Like the house built on the rock, there may be a down turn in the economy, the rain may fall, the winds may blow, the floods may come but your success will stand.

Principle-centered leaders have their sense of worth and security from within

You can build your esteem on many things. Many of us build our esteem on relationships, material possessions or the opinions of other people. Money and titles determine some people's self-esteem. When you obey principles, material acquisitions or achievements do not determine your sense of worth. Those things are temporary. Your sense of success and esteem must come from within.

We need leaders today, who like Jesus Christ, will not be under pressure to accumulate material wealth or to do extraordinary things just to prove that they are powerful. When you live in a society where you need to prove you are successful by owning a luxury car, you must let principles guide you. There are fraudsters driving such cars around town too. True success comes from your character.

I used to feel inferior to people who had larger organizations when mine was small. I used to feel inferior to people who owned better suits than I did. Who said that the value of a human being was in his suit? There are good men who do not have good suits yet. Real success begins from the inside. The more you obey principles, the more fulfillment you have; then the more faith builds in your heart about the outcome of your objectives.

We need to have our values corrected. We have to show a good example. We are stepping up to a higher level. The days of compromise with mediocre standards are over; we choose to do it God's way. From today, when your name is mentioned, it will 'sound' good; it will ring of integrity, reliability, trustworthiness and humility. I pray that through you, the fragrance of good character will spread in your organization and nation. I pray that as you align with principles, you will experience a new level of spiritual authority.

Do not compare yourself with others. There is a tendency to feel like failures when we compare ourselves with other people. God created you as a unique person. You cannot define success in your life by comparing your life with that of somebody else. You can be free from pressure. Principles are seeds and it takes time for a seed to turn into a harvest. Give principles time to produce results in your life.

Principle-centered leaders commit to personal development for life

Only heaven has the record of how many buckets, filled with water, that I carried on my head as a teenager in Africa. I understand what it means to use toothpaste and to squeeze every single drop of paste out of the tube. Sometimes I searched through the pockets of my shirts and pants, and even books in the hope that I would come across some money that I had forgotten. Many people who come around me today cannot imagine that I experienced all that and more. I have experienced transformation, and the key has been information.

I have discovered the principles that guarantee success, for example, sowing and reaping. Like I explained earlier, with just a bowl of corn seeds in my hand, I can tap into that law to create a future. Harvest time for corn comes in ninety days, and I harvest a lot more than I planted. To multiply the harvest again, wisdom tells me to increase the quantity of seed. With that, I create another cycle of success. Of course, if I do that consistently for years I will become rich. I can think this way because of what I have read. Leaders are readers.

I have experienced transformation, and the key has been information.

The principle-centered leader commits to personal development.

They read and what they read creates changes in their lives. What you do not know may be killing you. My mentor says that nobody has a unique mountain blocking his path; every man's ignorance is his mountain. What makes a difference between a human being and an animal? It is the capacity for knowledge. Animals have instinct but they do not have knowledge, so they do whatever they feel like doing. A human being has instinct and knowledge; that knowledge controls his instinct. That is why he does not relieve himself anytime and anywhere. It is knowledge that tells him some things are right while others are inappropriate. A human being without knowledge can behave like an animal.

I want you to get hungry for principles; you cannot plan for marriage and not read books on marriage. You cannot desire to prosper financially and not read books or attend seminars on financial success. How do you make rapid progress in your career without getting information that will help you?

You act to the best of your knowledge per time. You can switch from seeking revenge to offering forgiveness. If you are having problems relating with people, you need to know something about relationships that you have not known before. For example, I read "How to Win Friends and Influence People" by Dale Carnegie when I found it difficult to start and to sustain conversations. I acquired new skills and improved. Every leader needs to improve his or her management and leadership skills continually. A leader must never be too old to learn.

You act to the best of your knowledge per time.

Principle-centered leaders focus more on giving than on receiving

The essence of leadership is service. The measure of a leader's success is in contribution not acquisition. What is the problem with leadership in Africa? Culturally, leaders are served more than they serve.

"It is more blessed to give than to receive."[1] If you are a political, business or religious leader, focus on giving not receiving. The more you rise in leadership the more you realize how many resources are at your disposal.

If you do not deal with your greed, you may lose your credibility. My mentor said to me many years ago, "don't raise money; raise men." Over the years, I have come to appreciate that piece of advice.

On the day we all stand before God to give account of our lives, I sense there will be heavy regret by some leaders who come to realize how they squandered unusual opportunities to affect people's lives. Being the president of a country for example, is an opportunity most people will never have. Those who have such an opportunity should add value to people's lives. The greatest investments we will ever make in this world will be the value we add to people's lives. Leaders are givers.

Principle-centered leaders take on responsibility

Most people do not know how to succeed. When you have discovered the principles that guarantee success, and you have applied them with results to show, it is time to apply those principles to solve problems for others. When you know the principle of vision, you will use it for the benefit of an organization or nation. If you have financial management skills, you will use it to help many people.

David the King, in the Bible, had experienced God's protection while tending his father's sheep. When he saw Goliath messing up with Israel's army, he took Goliath on. He assumed responsibility for a whole nation. You may think you are small but when God's power works through you, extraordinary things happen. David was a young shepherd boy in obscurity, but God brought him to center stage.

You may not have a famous family name; you may not have gone to an Ivy League school. If you will take on the issues confronting your community or country, God will use you to solve unusual problems in unusual ways. He will use you beyond your wildest imagination. And in case you have a popular family name, remember that name was earned because of unusual impact on the community. Take it to a higher level.

Principle-centered leaders are proactive not reactive

The rule for managing relationships used to be, "An eye for an eye, and a tooth for a tooth."[2] Jesus brought a higher principle; "If someone slaps you on your right cheek turn the other to him also."[3] As a leader, you cannot live your life as a reaction. You must seize the opportunity . You cannot wait until conditions are perfect before you do what you need to do.

Principle-centered leaders act with courage

They understand the Law of Cause and Effect, so they act to create the conditions that will make their dreams realizable. They do not wait for things to happen, they make things happen. They are proactive.

People do many things as a reaction to perceived difficulties, scarcity or threats in their environment. Some cheat in exams as a reaction to the scarcity of positions. Others give or take bribe as a way of reacting to the scarcity of opportunities. Please do not live your life as a reaction. Do not yield control of your destiny to circumstances. Act in obedience to the principles that will create success for you.

Principle-centered leaders live balanced lives

God hates unjust weights; He does not like a life to lean to one side. He expects us to grow like Jesus in wisdom (mental development and skill acquisition); stature (physical development), favor with God (spiritual development), and favor with men (social development). True success comes with a balance.

Our goals should cover our spiritual lives, our families, and relationships with others, our careers and our health. Applying the principles of success in one area should not give us an excuse for breaking God's laws in another. God is not the author of confusion.

Characteristics of Unprincipled Leaders

Political expediency dictates their actions

I have heard it said that in politics there are no permanent friends and no permanent enemies, only permanent interests. Some people do whatever the situation demands for them to get results per time. The end justifies the means. They are unpredictable. As it is said, "If you don't stand for something, you will fall for anything." They are not principled in their approach to life. They do not have high moral standards. Ultimately, they disappoint the people they lead.

They favor people over principles and policies

They recruit based on favoritism instead of competence. They recruit relations or friends rather than the best man or woman for the job. Principles suffer because such leaders do not want to offend people. Such organizations never last. When you are a leader, you must give people priority over systems, but you must also give truth priority over persons.

Leadership that does not run on principles breeds greed

Financial gain and power for its own sake are the greatest aspirations of a leader who is not principled. Most people do not know how to succeed legitimately especially in career and business. Therefore, they are vulnerable to resorting to scheming. When such a person steps into a position of leadership it is seen as the best chance of a lifetime. If someone leaves a position of leadership without acquiring enough to fend for himself and his family for the rest of his life, some will consider such a person a fool. Unfortunately, the purpose of leadership is defeated. We are unable to leverage our collective potential to overcome our challenges and create development.

Characteristics of Principle-Centered Leadership

It gives everybody equal opportunity

The principles created by God do not differ for other people. God is not partial. When you build your leadership on principles, you cannot show favoritism either. That is the vision I have for my country, Nigeria. Someday, ethnicity will not matter, each citizen will have the opportunity to dream and to fulfill their dreams because there will be an equal platform for everyone.

This change has to begin with you and me. Start by letting go of every prejudice so you can serve your generation and the ones to come without limitation. As a leader, you should not favor a rich person over a poor person. Honor everyone. Once you begin to create class segregation, you will fail in leadership. You need to pay more attention to people who do not have. If you understand the purpose of power, you will rise to the highest levels of leadership. The greatest purpose of power is to create equality in the society. Seek to empower the powerless and protect the most vulnerable. For example, we need to protect the children and those with disabilities.

If you understand the purpose of power, you will rise to the highest levels of leadership. The greatest purpose of power is to create equality in the society.

The genocide in Rwanda demonstrated what eventually happens when leaders do not lead by principles and want to favor one tribe over the other. It breeds distrust and constant friction. Then one tribe tries to wipe out another. In your family, organization, unit or group, put principles over mundane things. It will give you capacity for vision. Prejudice makes a person narrow-minded.

It rewards productivity and positive attitudes

When some people join an organization, they quickly find out the power centers, that is, the powerful people there who have the ears of the boss. Then they begin to play their cards. They become sycophants, trying to impress the authorities. However, when you have a principle-centered leader, there is no tolerance for sycophancy.

I learnt early in my career that performance would always win over politics. I told myself that whatever happens I would stay on principles because that is the only place that has a future no matter the political or environmental threats that opposed me. The fact that someone made unkind remarks and hates you does not mean you should react. If you do, you will also fail. It is better to respond with love. Your business is to stay on the principles. They do not fail.

The United States of America will fulfill its potential only if there is an alignment with principles. The present system may seem to frustrate the person who wants to do things right while aiding the corrupt. When you walk straight, you expose the failure and lack of character of people with dubious intentions. Please take a stand all the same. A good name is better than great riches. We will all be better for it.

It believes in people

When you look at the principles of God, the central theme in God's relationship with man is love. Principle-centered leaders love people, believe in people and do not react to their weaknesses. They recognize and respond to their potential. When you choose to align with principles, integrity requires you to confront your own weaknesses. Man's fallen nature does not have the capacity to obey God. You will need the help of God to love people when they do crazy things.

When God looks at us, He remembers that we are dust; He knows how frail we are. God is not surprised when human beings fail. Some people think God is wicked and holds a hammer waiting for them to break His laws so He can hit them on the head. Actually, God is very merciful and can empathize with us. In fact, in order to communicate His empathy, He sent His Son to take on human flesh and to go through everything that we go through. Leaders, who lead by principles, do not react to people's weaknesses rather they relate to their potentials.

Chapter Seven
UNLEASH
YOUR LEADERSHIP
POTENTIAL

When you look at a seed and you have insight and foresight, you see beyond the seed. You see the tree and the fruits that will come from it. You see the forest that will evolve as you repeat this cycle over time. A seed has the potential to become a forest.

I like the word 'understanding.' When you look at the word, it seems to describe the thing that is under what is standing. It takes wisdom to discern the cause that has produced a particular effect. With that we are able to recreate success over and over.

Now, to the big discovery: the key to the release of your leadership potential is service. It is about solving problems for people and meeting needs in people's lives. It is unfortunate that today, many leaders in politics, in business and even in church ministry have still not gotten this fact.

It is an irony that some people who understand it have selfish motives. Some are even uneducated, yet they have influence. When you really look into it, what is the secret? It is the ability to cook for the hungry. It is the ability to give people little stipends to sustain them in hard times. Some even dispense drugs and analgesics to people who are sick. Do you know that malaria kills more people than HIV in Africa? Some leaders feel they are too sophisticated to offer basic services like that. Unfortunately, they blow a lot of hot air but have little influence.

Do you have a vision to become a CEO or a millionaire? That is great, but why do you want to become a millionaire? Why do you want to make money from the stock market? Why do you want to own real estate? Why do you want to be rich? Why do you want to be a governor or president? Is it all about you becoming powerful or living in luxury? I understand the desperation to be wealthy if one is from an impoverished background. Life can be very harsh when you are poor. Your humanity is devalued. It seems like a curse to be a child. The society treats you like a non-entity. You want to grow up quickly to escape oppression, and to have a chance to lord it over some people too. However, that kind of leadership has taken us more steps backward than forward. Here are some tips that will help you unleash your leadership potential.

Focus on People

In the bid to be successful, I had been oblivious to the fact that the people I was leading needed to be successful also. People have become increasingly suspicious of pastors and there must be a reason. Sometimes pastors do not realize that church members can read the desperation in their messages. There are times when a pastor belabors a revelation and the ultimate motive becomes clear; it is all about money. While it is certain that the ministry will have needs, the focus should be the people. People come to spiritual leaders to have their problems solved not to solve the problem of the spiritual leader. Leaders succeed only to the extent that they help other people to succeed. If you add value to people's lives, you will get money in return. Dr. David Oyedepo once said to me; "My definition of a millionaire is someone who has affected a million lives."

Have Genuine Compassion

You must have genuine compassion for people. Love and selfishness cannot work together. The focus of love should not be self; it should be the other person. Leadership is about giving, serving and solving problems. It is about meeting people's needs. If you love genuinely then you should be able to aptly detect what people really need. As a church minister, I used to think that having a beautiful building and the latest musical equipment and public address system were the greatest requirements for success. I was surprised to realize that those things will not guaranty that people will come or join the church. The big question I had not asked was: What do people really need? If this essence of leadership is grasped, it is applicable in all spheres of life.

Leaders succeed only to the extent that they help other people to succeed.

A political leader cannot make a good connection with people without identifying their needs. Nobody will really succeed in business legitimately without identifying people's needs. That is what leadership is about. My suggestion is if you really love people, pay attention to them. Listen to them, watch them and engage your intuition to identify exactly what they need. To do that, you must value people over money and power.

Identify and Meet People's Needs

As a public speaker and preacher, I enjoy teaching. Sometimes I feel that I have given a powerful lecture, but who should do the assessment? Of course, it should be the listener. What problem did the lecture solve for them? What need did the teaching meet in their lives?

My approach to teaching on finances changed the day it dawned on me that all I had been teaching was that people should give what they had. The teachings were valid from the standpoint of scriptures, but it was obvious the congregation did not even have the money. Was I really solving problems for the people? Something was missing. I prayed; "Lord, is there anything in the Bible that can show people how to make money?" If I could teach them how to make money legitimately, then they would have what to give. I began to get waves of practical insights. They resulted in my writing the books 'Start with What You Have,' 'Ideas Rule the World' and 'The Parable of Dollars.' The information in them comprises of simple principles that people apply everyday to create wealth but which people are sometimes not aware are in the Bible. The testimonies of change in people's lives have been outstanding.

My point is that you can succeed beyond your wildest imagination if you will take your mind off yourself and focus on others. If you want to lead, be a problem solver. As you rise in status, never lose this secret. Be willing to come down to the lowest level to offer service. Occasionally, as the boss, come to the ground floor and connect directly with your staff and clients, because selling is the lifeblood of any business.

I love the quality of service that I enjoy when I am in some parts of the world. I see many products and services that solve problems for me, and I do not mind paying at all when I can afford them. It is simply because those who create them are able to identify needs. I refer again to the GPS system in our cars. It's just more convenient to drive around without having to ask people for direction every few blocks. You program your destination and it takes you there, giving you accurate directions on the map with voice prompts. Well, it may have been invented for the use of the military, but some people had the rest of us in mind as well. They should be getting some little reward for being so caring.

There are too many opportunities for you and I to improve people's lives. The world is not a perfect place yet. You certainly have no business being broke. You need to invent and produce products and services to meet people's needs. Those needs are not complex. In fact, it is when you get too complex in your thinking that you miss them.

The essence of the release of supernatural resources is service. When Jesus received spiritual power, He used it to solve problems for the community. He affected the health sector, fed the hungry and educated the masses. It's time to break free from self-centeredness and lift the quality of life for the people around us. When I focused on myself, believing I had some special problems caused by curses, I could not release my leadership potential. I did not realize I had the power of blessing to distribute to others. Once I changed the focus from myself to others, I became motivated. When I see how devalued the lives of people in the developing parts of the world are, I cannot be silent. There is fire in my bones. I cannot have knowledge that has helped me and not put it at the disposal of the average person. I may not be able to do everything but I can do something. You too can do something. Let us get to work. Remember, it all begins where you are now, in your family, school, and neighborhood, or on your job.

If you want to lead, be a problem solver.

As long as you see yourself as a victim, believing that you are the one in need, God cannot use you to meet needs. Go ahead and be a blessing to others. Stop running after people to seek help; some people need to be running after you. Refuse to be a liability; you are an asset.

Most people who do not have money think money is man's greatest need. They end up with low self-esteem not realizing that people who have money still have needs in their lives. There are people who have money but do not have a good marriage. Others have houses but do not have good health. You may not have money to give but you may be able to solve a problem for them with the power of God or a piece of information from your personal experience. Whichever way, you cannot call yourself cursed when God wants to use you to break curses on people's lives. Offer yourself as a solution provider, a servant of all. Start with your family. Identify their needs and be a blessing to them. Then you can be a blessing to your neighbors, and then at work.

I pray that God will open your eyes to identify the unique problems you are equipped to solve for humanity and that He will give you ideas to solve them.

Chapter Eight
LEADERSHIP
AND CHANGE

Things are changing around us and they are changing quickly. Some people ignore change and that is a problem. Change is inevitable. Things change, whether for good or for bad.

Change is inevitable. Somebody said that the only permanent thing in life is change. Some people ignore change while some others accept, prepare and do their best to manage it. My challenge here is; it is not enough to accept that change is inevitable, prepare to adapt. When you are a leader, you actually do not wait for change to happen; you make it happen. You initiate change. The ultimate test of leadership is the ability to create change.

On the global scene, there is a restructuring of economies. New economic giants are emerging. Technology is advancing. The climatic patterns are changing. All of these things impact us in different ways.

These changes have implications for individuals, organizations and nations. Not all change is considered improvement; but without change, there cannot be improvement. Those who are praying for improvement in the economy and in government should understand the implication of their prayers. If there will be improvement, there has to be change. I challenge you as a part of your family or organization, to be the change champion. Change is inevitable and the person who sees it, catches and helps bring it to life or create it is the leader. If you will fulfill your destiny as a leader, do not sit down and wait for change to happen. Make change happen.

If you have ever been to the beach, you will notice those powerful waves that surge from the ocean. It is important to know that we cannot create those waves; God creates them. Nonetheless, we can surf waves and ride on them. Likewise, God sends waves of change to us and we must learn to catch the tides when those waves come. Instead of trying to protect our position and to stay in our comfort zones, holding on to past success, it is important that we jump out, set sail and go on a voyage to a land we have not discovered.

Make change happen.

I believe that God is not through with you yet. There is a new level for you to attain. Some people have held on to past revelations without realizing that yesterday's revelation can become today's tradition. It is one thing for you to know what God said; it is another to know what God is saying. Usually, to maximize the effect of a revelation, we build an organization, but the vision can become stranded if the organization cannot adapt to change. Like dinosaurs that became extinct because they could not adapt to changes in the environment, many organizations are old shelves of their old selves. Change is inevitable. To experience lasting success, especially as leaders, change must be our friend. Let us consider ways to develop the ability to lead change.

Have A Dream Of The Future

When you are a leader, you must be able to create a picture of a better future, and communicate it to the people on your team. You need to have a powerful vision; a vision that makes blood boil in your own veins and in other people's veins. It must be able to motivate you to hit the ground running every morning.

So then, how do you capture the vision? If you are not seeing something new, new victories, expansion, enlargement, increase, growth, everything will soon come to a halt. It is vision that makes a leader. For instance, if you take one leader out and bring another in, a team that was dying can come alive. What gives life is the capacity for vision. It is vision that gives a leader magnetic power. The potential to capture the future is rare. So when people find someone who can predict the future with certainty, they want to be around the person because they know the future is inevitable. Where there is no vision, there are no leaders.

A vision gives hope, direction and motivation. It breeds persistence and attracts provision. The dreams of today are the realities of tomorrow. The best time to shape tomorrow is today, because like fluid it is ever changing. The place where we do the molding is in our imagination.

Share the Vision

This sounds easy. It should happen naturally but it does not happen like that. Not many people know exactly how to communicate a vision to the extent that people are willing to follow them to create the change. Share the vision especially with the people you are leading. Tell them where you are going.

One thing is important; we have to help people see how they fit into the vision. Sometimes, people find it difficult to flow with a vision because they do not see how it connects with their life. In communicating the vision, you must answer this important question; "What is in it for them?" Everybody's internal radio is tuned to a frequency; WII FM-'What's in it for me?' You do not get people's attention until you tell them how your vision will benefit them.

I remember when I announced to our church members that our attendance was going to grow from five hundred to two thousand people. I expected the whole church to be excited about it, but they just looked at me. I wondered what I did wrong. A church member walked up to me after that service and explained how the new crowd would change the dynamics of our church. The new crowd would be more in number than existing members. She said it would not be as easy for old members to walk up to me to discuss after services, like they did then. That was enlightening. So, while I was excited by the prospect of growth for the church, they were thinking how the growth would affect them.

The next Sunday I said, "Praise God, our church is going to grow to two thousand. There is a large crowd out there that is coming in, and those who are coming are even more than those who are here. Some of you have been praying for husbands or wives and it seems your prayers have not been answered. I am glad to let you know that your husbands or wives may be part of those who are coming. Everybody shouted, "Amen! The lesson: put what is important to the people in the vision. It doesn't matter how grand your idea is if you don't know how to communicate it.

Identify and Challenge Limiting Assumptions and Traditions

People naturally resist change. To weaken resistance to change, we must deal with the underlying assumptions and traditions. Once you do that, the resistance to change will be limited.

People tend to expect success to come the same way twice,

but God is original. He brings our miracles in creative ways. Unwritten rules keep us from reaching our potentials, and we have many of them. If you will do anything special with your life, you will have to break many of those rules. There are rules you should not break though; do not break God's laws, but be flexible enough if you are going to walk with God, to break rules, especially those unwritten ones.

For instance, it is normal for churches to run special events like seminars and conventions. That's been the tradition and most never question it. Please, do not get me wrong. There is nothing wrong with these special events. I have had life changing experiences at conventions. However, at a point, we had a peculiar challenge. We were trying to get a new facility but could not afford it. I had to ask myself, "Who said you must run this event?" We cancelled the anniversary convention for that year. When I announced it at the pastors' meeting it was like, "What?" I said, "Where is it written in the New Testament, 'thou must do anniversary convention?'" Everybody understood what I was speaking about. It was just an assumption that had been made for such a long time it had become tradition. For the first time we were able to conserve funds. The next time we found a facility we paid for it within a few days.

We have exercised liberty in breaking many unwritten rules such as that one. We had to shorten the length of our services when we had more people than we had space. In fact, we had to change the order of the service and it felt like we were about to commit a sacrilege. The order of service in the average church is predictable, but there is no place in the New Testament where the order of a service is stated. I believe it is deliberately set up that way by the Holy Spirit to allow for flexibility.

If you will create new dimensions of impact through your leadership, you must think outside the box and make room for people who think differently. The more successful an organization is, the more there is a desire to preserve the

Where progress is desired, change is inevitable.

way the success was achieved. Excuse me; some of what got us to where we are cannot take us beyond where we are. We need new ideas. We must maintain our innovative ability. Sometimes you have mavericks on your team who tend to see things differently from everybody. They may seem like a pain, but they also bring some of the brightest ideas sometimes. An organization deeply steeped in tradition will frustrate such people. Sometimes people see them as rebels, but not all of them are rebels. The ones that are, you know what to do about them. If the devil is inside a man, try to get the devil out of him, but if you cannot get the devil out, get the man and the devil out.

To release our creative juices, we should ask, 'why?' "Why should we do it like that?" "Why shouldn't we do it this way?" We must challenge assumptions. We must challenge old proverbs. We need to challenge traditions and different aspects of culture. Jesus would say to people; "You have heard that it has been said, but I say to you." He was challenging old assumptions and traditions. The practices that run on lasting principles and values should not change. The ones that are not should change. The practices that run on principles, but which are no longer relevant should go. Where progress is desired, change is inevitable.

Chapter Nine
SHARE THE POWER

Personal transformation does not go to completion in a day, it happens daily. It happens by the law of sowing and reaping. In just a few years, the seeds of leadership sown into your heart will yield fruit. You will experience unusual opportunities to lead. You will grow in influence. When that happens, please share the power with others.

We exist today because of a desire in God's heart to delegate His authority. God had a vision and He decided that He was not going to do it alone. He decided to have people that He would share His power with, who would help in the fulfillment of His vision. That is why we exist. He had created other beings before, but of course, none of them could function to the level He wanted them to because they did not have the talent. He decided to create beings in His own class to help Him do the job. Take note that because you have the nature of God in you, you should also have the desire to raise people to your level to help you do what you intend to do.

Today, instead of giving out power like God did, people tend to hoard it. That has been one of the major reasons for the slow pace of development in some countries. It affects families, businesses and churches too. It causes failure in leadership. The best way to keep power is to give it away.

Until you let go of what is in your hand you cannot receive something new. Until you let go of what you are doing now and give it to someone else, you cannot move on to a higher level of influence. To believe that there is no one else who can do what you are doing now is self-deception. The person who delegates authority and shares power; who recruits and brings somebody else along; who teaches someone to do what he or she has learnt to do, that person will rise faster in leadership than the one who finds it difficult to let go.

There are things you will never be able to do, and there are potentials in you that you will never realize until you share your power and influence with others. Remember God said: "It is not good for a man to be alone." [1]

Until you let go of what is in your hand you cannot receive something new.

In my study of church growth for almost three decades, I have come to realize that most churches never grow large. Most churches have less than two hundred members. When the attendance hits between a hundred and two hundred people, the growth stops. Something fundamental must change for you to break that barrier, and I sought to find out how. Interestingly, when I began to study entrepreneurship, I discovered that in the business world, the average business also stagnates between the second and third year. A University[2] that researched on it named that phenomenon the 'brick wall'. The brick wall is a stronghold most people never break through, but you can scale the brick wall. I discovered that the reason businesses stall is exactly the same reason churches stall in growth.

In the process of growth, a business requires resources beyond the personal abilities of the founder. One person can no longer afford the skills, temperaments, time, wisdom and knowledge required. If the business owner does not quickly design a system, hire other people to come in, and leave some of those areas that require specialization to people who are better skilled, the business owner will suffer a burnout. It is at this stage that a business owner's health begins to fail because one person cannot be CEO, Finance Manager, Administration Manager, Production Manager, Sales and Marketing Manager, Purchasing and Supply Officer, Accountant, Secretary, Office Assistant and Chauffeur of a large organization at the same time.

If you do not delegate power, you are limited in your capacity to receive assignments from God.

D. L. Moody is reported to have said that he would rather put ten men to work than do the work of ten men. Many businesses which were founded by people with technical expertise, but who did not have the required management and leadership skills have fizzled out. If you do not delegate power, you are limited in your capacity to receive assignments from God. What I mean is that you can trust someone who has twenty people to help him do a job with more assignments than the person who does it alone. The person who has twenty people helping him has greater volume to get the job done.

Similarly, research has established that a pastor cannot personally manage more than two hundred people, if he has to conduct services, do the preaching, visit them, conduct their weddings and so on. That is why the growth in attendance stalls. To break that barrier, he or she must pick some of those two hundred members and teach them to do the job as well as he can. If twenty of them grow as leaders and have the capacity to attract and manage fifty people each then the amount of growth is one thousand people. The potential for growth increases geometrically. We must empower people.

The first time Nike (my wife) and I went on vacation together, some of our members were apprehensive. They were afraid there would be a drastic reduction in attendance in our absence. We took the risk anyway, and the opposite happened. We were out for only two weeks, and the attendance increased while we were away. If you think nobody can do what you do except you, you may realize how far off the mark you are after you have extended yourself and circumstances force you to relinquish control. It is better to delegate willingly than to be forced to do so by adverse circumstances.

WHY WE DO NOT DELEGATE

Insecurity and the fear of losing authority

"If I give the power to somebody else then I would have nothing, I would become irrelevant." These thoughts are what most leaders think, but it does not work like that. It works in the opposite. In fact, the more you give, the more you get. Share the power because you are not going to make much progress if you do not allow other people to advance.

Fear of the job being done poorly

We tend to forget that we were not born with all the skills that we have now. We are afraid someone would not do the job as well as we can. All that we know is all we have learned. Let us allow others to learn and make mistakes. We can correct them and let them try again. Such investments of trust, money, time and patience in people yield tremendous returns.

Fear of the job being done better

How would you feel if someone that you trained becomes more proficient on the job? If you feel a tinge of envy, it will be understandable. We are human. Some leaders cannot handle it, so they do not give people the opportunity to express themselves. But if someone you train can now do the job at an extraordinary level that is to your credit. That should be the objective of leadership in the first place.

Lack of training

Plain and simple, many leaders have never attended a training program on delegation. We just do not know how to go about it, usually because nobody mentored us. We can set it as an objective. Moses didn't know how to do it until his father-in-law taught him[3].

Impatience

It takes a lot of patience to train people. They have to take their baby steps, make mistakes and try again. If you do not delegate, you may seem to turn out good quality work quickly, but you will have to slow down when the job is more than you can handle and you do not have people to help you do it. Give people time to grow.

BENEFITS OF DELEGATION

You have time to pray and think

As a leader, the one skill you should develop is the ability to prioritize.

When you are a leader, you better know that the basic resources you have to work with are intangible. Catching a vision and planning how to turn it to reality is your job. Remember, it is vision that makes a leader; but when you are too involved in the routine jobs, running up and down, you do not have time to make internal progress. When you "stand still" within, you will eventually "stand still" without. You have to delegate so you can concentrate on your most important tasks. You cannot leave prayer, meditation and strategic thinking to subordinates. As a leader, the one skill you should develop is the ability to prioritize.

You can communicate the vision with clarity

There is a way you have to communicate vision for people to get it. The most important thing in communicating your vision is clarity. If you do not focus on the big picture, you cannot help people to see it. Avoid distraction and focus your powers like a laser beam on your purpose.

You can focus on recruitment and training of leaders

The Pareto principle suggests that, "80% of your result comes from 20% of the people you work with."[4] You have to learn to spend 80% of your time with the top 20% of the people you lead. Those are your delighted leaders; those are the people who make things happen. One of them is worth the work of twenty, a hundred or even a thousand people. You maximize the use of your time when you invest it in them.

There is growth

In the scriptures, the disciples of Jesus had a situation where some people were over-looked in the distribution of food. There was resentment. Rather than add that to their business of running the whole system, the disciples appointed seven men with character and competence and delegated the job to them. The result was geometric growth[5]. You can experience the same thing in business. That is the essence of this book. The more we focus on producing leaders by teaching and imparting leadership skills, the greater our potential for growth and impact.

I challenge you today, whatever you know, teach someone, however little you think it is. That is the beginning of leadership. Do not die with your knowledge. Do not let heaven regret divine investments in your life. Pass the knowledge on. "The liberal soul shall be made fat. He that waters others shall be watered also himself."[6] As you help other people to rise, God will lift you.

Please reproduce yourself. Do not be the lone ranger champion. If everything collapses, and everyone is stuck just because you are not around, do not brag about it. It is not an achievement.

You can become addicted to power the way someone gets addicted to hard drugs. It can be intoxicating. At that point, it is difficult to let go of it. Please, share the power. Let somebody else taste it. Let them enjoy it the same way you do. I know that success can seem scarce so when you get it, you do not want to take risks with it. However, the day you cannot do it yourself you will be frustrated. If it is a car, you better not be the only one who knows how to operate that sophisticated car because the day you need someone else to do the driving you will be stuck. Let somebody else sit in the driver's seat and feel the power.

Reproduce yourself. Raise a mentor. There is no success without a successor and we do not really know how successful you are as a leader until you are not around.

Chapter Ten
CHOOSING GOOD LEADERS

The greatest need in the world today is leadership. I will mention a few facts about choosing leaders, beginning with character.

People Get the Kind of Leader They Deserve

The responsibility for choosing leaders in most parts of the world falls on the followers. The quality of the people therefore largely determines the quality of leaders they get. I did not think this way before, but seeing the way elections go at times, I have learnt a few lessons.

When I began to speak on the radio some years ago, I suddenly realized that I had the opportunity to speak to many people, and that I could address those in government through the broadcast. Sometimes, when I wrote my script, I felt like confronting people in public office over issues that bothered me, but I heard the voice of the Holy Spirit inside me; "Hold it! Do not bother about those in government, talk to the people. Check your history; whenever good people have tried to rule, it has been easy to remove them from government. The leadership comes out of the base so do not expect that good people will come out of a corrupt base. Talk to the people; when they change, the quality of leadership will change."

It took me time to wrap my brain around it, but now I am convinced that largely, followers determine the quality of leadership, and leaders in turn determine the quality of lives of their followers. That is the equation because everything rises and falls on leadership. Of course, there are extraneous factors like colonization, slavery and autocratic leadership structures that have forced leadership on people in some places.

In the Bible, Moses chose twelve top class leaders from the twelve tribes of Israel to check out Canaan. Out of the twelve, ten came back with a bad report while two gave a good report[1]. Majority of the Israelites decided to line up behind the ten leaders who had a negative attitude. They had a choice. They were not compelled to accept the negative report given by the majority, but they did. "Let us select a leader who will take us back to slavery," they said[2]. They craved for negative leadership because there was an alignment between their values and attitudes and the values and attitudes of those ten leaders. If their values and attitudes had aligned with the report of the two who were positive, they would have followed those two.

Nike and I had the opportunity of speaking with a highly respected church leader in Nigeria. We met on an international flight and I asked his opinion on the church's role in the country's situation. His response was quite interesting. He said; "People get the kind of leaders they deserve. Let us continue to pray and preach to people, so we can have more righteous people in the country. When righteous people become the majority, we will tilt the scale. You will see that it will reflect automatically in the leadership." Maybe he saw the puzzled look on my face. Then he added, "If you ask a group of thieves to choose a leader, they will never choose a policeman." Now, that was profound. Then I thought to myself that if you force the police officer on them and they have the right to impeach him, they would do that quickly.

With all the miracles that had happened in the desert between Egypt and the Promised Land, majority of the Israelites still had the mindset of slavery, inferiority, mediocrity and poverty that they had developed in Egypt. It was so easy for them to align with the ten leaders who were pessimistic. Joshua and Caleb who gave a positive report had a different mindset entirely. To help people desire higher quality leadership, leaders need to give their followers a new sense of identity. As a leader, you need to help them break free from low self-esteem. When they are free in their minds, they will not endure oppressors as leaders.

THE VALUE SYSTEM

Change Their Mindset

You need to change the mindset of those you lead. You need to change their concept of and expectations from leadership, in order to experience significant change. Whether you lead a family, organization or in government, this is where to start. There is no leadership without improvement, and people will not experience sustainable progress without a change in their thinking.

God Keeps Away Good Leaders from Wayward Nations

At a point in the history of Israel, God took away the wealth of the nation and all the skilled professionals[3]. When a people reject the principles and the values of God, He keeps away good leaders from them. We must watch over the spiritual health of those we lead and of the nation as a whole. Please listen to those you are leading. Are their conversations positive? Do they have the 'can do' spirit? Do they value principles? Have they adopted the core values of the group?

Intercession

There is a place for intercession. Those of us that have influence, with God, can create a new future for our nation, recovering lost opportunities. In the history of ancient Israel, the process of movement from Egypt to Canaan seemed like it was going to fail but Moses through intercession created a new process and a new future[4]. Human nature is complex. Sometimes people do not know why they behave the way they do. We can access power beyond human ability for them and for ourselves. Through spiritual warfare, we can pull down mental strongholds. Anyone who has experienced a change of mindset knows that changing your thinking is warfare.

Faith and Attitude

Faith and attitude differentiate between the people who fail and those who do not. This we see again in the movement of Israel from Egypt to Canaan. Those who were positive made it in, though they were few. Most countries have gone through seasons of struggle before they were able to set their systems on sound principles. However in every instance, some people provided strong leadership and challenged the people to be positive. As a leader, you must be an incurable optimist, and your optimism must be contagious. All things are possible to him that believes.

The Place of Patience

When Martin Luther King Jr. declared his dream for the future of America, he knew it would take time. Some visions are trans-generational. God made a promise to Abraham that he would have a son through Sarah. It took time for it to happen. In fact, some of the things God showed Abraham took centuries to come into manifestation. Moses received a new vision for Israel, but it was going to take time to materialize. It took forty years. Our own process of change may not be as long as that but it will take time. Like a seed, give your vision of change time to materialize.

Strategy: Faith and Vision

As long as you believe that things cannot change, you will compromise with the existing corrupt or mediocre system. Your vision will always affect your behavior. If your vision does not affect your behavior, it is not a vision; it is an illusion. If you live by faith and have vision, your life will have impact. Take the long look, and position yourself for its manifestation.

Real leadership

A position does not make you a leader; it only gives you the opportunity to lead. The most influential people in a country may not be those occupying political office. There are kings and there are kingmakers. Only one person can be governor at a time. You cannot say that because you are not the governor, you do not have the opportunity to be a leader. God put something inside you that can be a big blessing to this world. You are a leader when you use your gifts and skills to add value to people's lives. Find your place and be a blessing.

Catch Them Young

We have to pray for the young people. Two or three elections from now, they will be old enough to cast their votes. It will be too late to try to influence their thinking two months to the elections. We must start their programming now. We must give the youth visions and dreams of a great future, especially because what they see and hear in the news makes the future look bleak to them. But when they get vision, they'll see the challenges around them as opportunities. Let us prepare them to be problem solvers with a global mindset.

Rescue the Educational System

Do you see what is happening to the educational system, especially the public school system? It is creating new cycles of spiritual slavery and poverty. Godlessness is being distributed wholesale. If you want to predict the future of a country, look at its school system. What goes into the mind comes out in a life. You and I can take responsibility for the schools in our communities whether our children attend them or not. They are a description of the future of our communities. We can intervene in formal and informal ways.

Choose To Live in the New Nation

For those of us who can see a new nation and a beautiful future in our dreams, our eyes will see it, we will taste it and we will touch it. Since I decided not to internalize my external environment but decided to capture great dreams for the future, I have seen God change my personal environment. I have raised the standard for myself. The kingdom (government) of God is real in my personal life. You will experience the transformation as you dream of a better future in your own life.

Prepare To Lead

Get ready because as change comes in the thinking of the people, and you adopt the principles and values that guarantee success, there will be opportunities for you to influence others as a leader. When darkness covers the earth, God's glory will shine even more brightly in your life. The world's problems and the challenges of your environment become your opportunities to influence others for good. The essence of leadership is service, meeting needs and solving problems. Somebody reading this will lead in business. Someone else will lead in the media. Another person will lead in sports. Others will lead in government, and some people will lead in church ministry. Prepare for your opportunities. God will help you to fulfill your destiny as a leader.

BOOK ENDNOTES

CHAPTER ONE

1. Genesis 1

2. John 5:19-20

CHAPTER TWO

1. Psalm 78:72

2. Maxwell, John. The 21 Irrefutable Laws of Leadership (Nashville: Thomas Nelson, 1998), the 1st law of leadership - The Law of the Lid. Pg. 1-10.

3. 1 Samuel 26: 1-25

4. Maxwell, John. The 21 Irrefutable Laws of Leadership (Nashville: Thomas Nelson, 1998). - The 16th Law of Leadership - The Law of Momentum Pg. 165-174

5. 1 Samuel 17

6. Mathew 16:24

CHAPTER THREE

1. Luke 9:62

2. Luke 14:28

3. Acts 20:35.

4. Isaiah 30:21

CHAPTER FOUR

1. Hybels, Bill (2002). Courageous Leadership. Grand Rapids, MI: Zondervan.

2. Proverbs 23:7a

3. Ecclesiastes 9:11

CHAPTER FIVE

1. 2 Chronicles 10:1- 17

2. Mathew 22: 39

3. Ephesians 5:25

4. Ephesians 5:22

5. 2 Kings 5: 1-27

6. 1 Samuel 12:1-3

7. Proverbs 16:32

CHAPTER SIX

1. Acts 20:35

2. Mathew 5:38

3. Mathew 5:39

CHAPTER NINE

1. Genesis 2:18

2. The 'brick wall' phenomenon was named by the graduate school of University of Michigan.

3. Exodus 18

4. The principle was suggested by management thinker Joseph M. Juran. It was named after the Italian economist Vilfredo Pareto, who observed that 80% of property in Italy was owned by 20% of the Italian population. Since J. M. Juran adopted the idea, it might better be called "Juran's assumption".

5. Acts 6:1-7

6. Proverbs 11:25

CHAPTER TEN

1. Numbers 13

2. Numbers 14:4

3. Isaiah 3: 1- 9

4. Numbers 14:11 - 24

FOR OTHER TITLES BY THE AUTHOR

Visit:

www.samadeyemi.net

www.successpower.tv

Sam
Adeyemi

BUILD
REAL
WEALTH

Practical Steps to Regain

Financial Stability

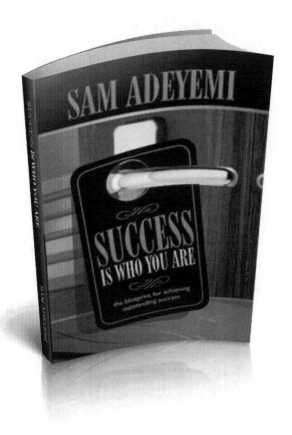

Made in the USA
Middletown, DE
23 August 2015